Lucky Buck

by Evan Allen
illustrated by Bob Brugger

Scott Foresman
is an imprint of

Glenview, Illinois • Boston, Massachusetts • Mesa, Arizona
Shoreview, Minnesota • Upper Saddle River, New Jersey

Every effort has been made to secure permission and provide appropriate credit for photographic material. The publisher deeply regrets any omission and pledges to correct errors called to its attention in subsequent editions.

Unless otherwise acknowledged, all photographs are the property of Pearson.

Photo locations denoted as follows: Top (T), Center (C), Bottom (B), Left (L), Right (R), Background (Bkgd)

Illustrations by Bob Brugger

Photograph 12 Corbis

ISBN 13: 978-0-328-39449-4
ISBN 10:   0-328-39449-1

Buck the duck was a fast swimmer. But the other ducks at the pond didn't like the way he swam. Every day they teased him. Buck dreamed of swimming like all the other ducks.

3

Buck woke up the next morning. He scrambled from his bed. He marched down through the gully to the pond in the valley.

"Today, I am going to learn to swim like other ducks," he said.

Buck shook his tail feathers. He shot into the water. "Head up! Neck up!" he shouted. "I can do it! I can stay up!"

Buck tried to sit tall. But his head and neck flopped. His beak skimmed the water. Buck darted between the reeds like a speeding surfboard.

Buck made himself sit up again. But after a few seconds, he flopped. Suddenly, he saw that the other ducks were watching him. *Oh, no!* he thought. *Here it comes!*

"Buck, you are a lame duck!" shouted Quack, the leader. "You will never swim the way we do! See you later, alligator!"

The others called out, "In a while, crocodile!" Buck put his beak to the water. He swam away as fast as he could.

Buck walked up onto the shore at the
other side of the pond. He sank down
into the mud. He put his head on a thatch
of grass. The teasing voices echoed in his
mind. Then Buck fell asleep.

Buck woke up and saw a duck standing next to him. "I coach the All Duck Swim Team," said the duck. "You are speedy!"

"I am an ugly swimmer," Buck said. "I look like an alligator when I swim."

"I think you're a beautiful swimmer," said the coach. "Will you join the team?"

Buck joined the team. He won every race that season. He was ahead by a beak every time!

Buck became famous for the way he swam. Now other ducks dreamed of swimming the way Buck did!

The All Duck Swim Team celebrated at the end of the season. The team members signed autographs for their fans.

Quack clutched Buck's autograph in his wings. "I want to swim the way you do, Buck," he said.

"I'll be happy to teach you!" said Buck.

Ducks in the Water

Ducks are born to swim. Their bodies are made to swim and dive easily in the water. Ducks have webbed feet that push them through the water. Their legs are located toward the backs of their bodies for balance.

Ducks' bodies make oil that coats their feathers. Water slides off the oil. Their skin stays dry while they are in the water.